£6·60

CW00742173

To Amuse a Shrinking Sun

PHOTOGRAPH: JOAN DIGBY

John Digby

To Amuse a Shrinking Sun
Poems & Collages

Anvil Press Poetry

Published in 1985
by Anvil Press Poetry Ltd
69 King George Street London SE10 8PX

ISBN 0 85646 138 5 hardback
ISBN 0 85646 139 3 paperback

Copyright © John Digby 1985

This book is published with
financial assistance from
The Arts Council of Great Britain

Photoset in Rockwell
by Bryan Williamson, Swinton, Berwickshire
Printed in Great Britain
by Camelot Press Ltd, Southampton

Acknowledgements

Some of these poems have appeared in *Dream Helmet, Durak, English and American Surrealist Poetry* (Penguin Books), *Jazz, Kayak, Magog, Montana Gothic, Pearl Magazine.*

To Chick-Chick

"And as I sat there brooding on the old, unknown world, I thought of Gatsby's wonder when he first picked out the green light at the end of Daisy's dock. He had come a long way to this blue lawn, and his dream must have seemed so close that he could hardly fail to grasp it. He did not know that it was already behind him, somewhere back in that vast obscurity beyond the city, where the dark fields of the republic rolled on under the night.

Gatsby believed in the green light, the orgastic future that year by year recedes before us. It eluded us then, but that's no matter—to-morrow we will run faster, stretch out our arms further . . . . And one fine morning—

So we beat on, boats against the current, borne back ceaselessly into the past."

F. Scott Fitzgerald, *The Great Gatsby*

Contents

Collages

Preface

Poetry and collage at first appear to be very different modes of expression, one verbal and the other pictorial. Yet for me their similarity has always been so striking that I cannot avoid emphasizing the likenesses. Despite the fact that poems are made with words, many strive for a concrete quality, sometimes in form, sometimes in imagery; and even the cutting that brings a poem to its final shape is an incisive process that relies, as collage does, on a certain finesse of edges.

In that statement I have consciously made collage a metaphor for poetic composition. I could just as easily have done the reverse and described how the collagist strives for poetic unity from disparate forms "yoked by violence together" (to quote Dr Johnson on the metaphysical poets). Like poetry, collage is a medium, often imagistic and allusive, sometimes narrative, and at other times abstract.

My collages began as extensions of my surreal poetry, and from the beginning I sensed a strong similarity in poetic and collage construction. Both take shape from pre-existing matter, in my case mostly dreams, expressed in words or pieces of paper that have a literal reality. Like poetry, collage is a process of shifting the literal into an imaginative space that expands its meaning into the figurative.

Imagination, I believe, is the faculty of discovery used to unearth something from the past. It is not unlike the Australian aborigines' "dream time" which has primacy over their actual waking life. Their real life lies in dreams recalled from a previous time almost lost in mists of history or snatched at briefly in dreams. Only by dreaming and concentrating on the imagination in order to deepen and broaden it can this former, truer existence be made real. In a sense it is like a form of magic; the more we imagine, the deeper the imagination becomes, until the conscious world appears as dim as a half-forgotten dream and the dream appears as real as the world in which we live.

To invent a world would be an escape from reality, but to acknowledge this "dream time" is to perpetuate a voyage of discovery and amazement. Both my collages and poems hope to suggest the essence and reality of this unconscious world.

When I first began to complement my poetry with collage, the figure of Dante guided by Virgil became a recurrent symbol of the shift from literal into symbolic space. In a sense all space is symbolic. Even the most natural spaces, the shapes of birds and animals or the woods in which we get lost, are vaster and more infinitely complex than their literal reality.

These are the images I keep returning to both in my poetry and collages. The origin of their personal meaning for me is in my childhood,

11

spent more profitably in London parks and the Zoo than the many schools I attended. I realized as a child that the only career I could imagine was that of zoo-keeper. So, at the age of fifteen I began working at Regents Park Zoo. Then as now birds were my keenest passion. According to my grandmother, "bird" was my first spoken word. I can still recall my own birth as a bird pulled fluttering from the darkness, and even now dreams of birds and animals rescue me from depression or sing against fear of extinction. I personally cannot imagine poetry or collage without birds and animals. A world without them would indeed be very sad. Beyond their literal and even figurative presence in my own work, they are models of lyric grace inextricably tied to my conception of imaginative unity. They are inseparable from their habitats, that is to say from their origins and ends.

Perhaps my concern with unity derives ultimately from the imagination's strong desire to witness origins and ends, though it pictures them differently in different media. The poem, whether structured by a narrative or by a gratuitous flow of images is, in the nature of language, temporal. The linear movement of syntax produces an order that becomes clear in time, as the reader reads.

Because poetry is a temporal medium I suppose that no visual image can hope to illustrate scenes witnessed by the poetic imagination. There are, of course, exceptions to the rule, and Blake comes foremost to mind. But for the most part, art seems to me to introduce a spatial sense that is complementary to the temporal movement of poetry. Art presents the imaginative event grasped at once as a unified impression.

For me, poetry and collage work together to express the time and space occupied by the imagination. In that sense they are structured from fragments of the same world and often share the same imagery. While most of the poems are narratives, their scenes of human dreaming often open into the landscape of natural history populated by my collage wildlife. The collages in turn allude back through the birds and animals to the environment altered by man. They also allude to books, for all of my collages are constructed from black and white line engravings derived from printed sources.

Thus my pictorial fragments are, so to speak, a visual vocabulary deliberately akin to typographical words, and in their tonal spectrum of greys and sepias I seek to discover the shades of connotation that give "colour" to the poet's language. Together the poems and collages are intended to be a single book rather than a book of poems decorated with collages.

John Digby
Oyster Bay, New York 1984

Lines to a Dead Thrush

Your eye
a delicate shade of brown
stares up vacantly
to a wide expanse of sky
in which swifts wheel and dip
beneath a traffic of passing clouds

broken neck wings legs
you are nothing now
but a bundle of crushed and matted feathers
decaying between railway-lines

I watch an army of ants crawl
between your wings
and over the torn flesh of your breast
where flies have already deposited their eggs

soon the long-tailed rats
will slither from their holes
dragging their bellies between the grass
along the embankment
in the quiet of the evening
sniffing at your rain-drenched remains

in time
even your skeleton will crumble
turn to a fine chalk
and scatter on the wind

nothing will remain
but an image of you
perched among the foliage
of a wind-wrapped tree
with your head flung back
hurtling your song
across the roar of the morning traffic

Then and Only Then

When Fra Filippo Lippi
was contemplating painting his Madonna and Child
telephones washing-machines televisions were exploding
eagles and hawks discarded their hair-shirts
and trees suddenly took to the air
strutting through space blazing with fire

when Leonardo da Vinci
was finishing his Virgin of the Rocks
we bound the hair of the pepper tree around our waists
placed the dolphin's eggs under the sun's pillow
and set sail for foreign shores
searching for the magical mirror
that would reflect our lost youth

when Piero Della Francesca drew the preliminary sketches
for his Baptism of Christ
the sun became a vast lake in which winged giraffes
appeared from the depths and reached up to nibble the stars
we knew then that the baker's bed was the elephant's dream
and the virgin abandoned her body to her lover
with the passion of a dead man tying up his shoes

when Jacopo Bassano
was adding the final touches to his Christ at Emmaus
we caught and knotted the trade winds around our throats
and sailed through the air on icebergs
radiating a heat so fierce that the sun sheltered behind
the gloved hands of a passing flock of whirling birds

when Giovanni Bellini
fell asleep over his finished Orpheus
life with its terrible speed
threw out blue flames shattering our shadows our bodies
and we awoke in a labyrinth echoing with strange music
then and only then we realized
that we had arrived on the other side of the mirror
where the darkness was an old friend
preparing the schooner for the voyage
to that domain where the marvellous sings its crystal odes

The Bears

These orange coloured bears
shaggy and cumbersome
their faces smeared with honey
slowly lumber forward on their hind legs
rising from the sleeper's unconsciousness
and begin their astonishing dance
a silent deliberate ballet
to a strange music splashed with silence
in which time has wound down to an adagio
in order to hold the dreamer's attention

each bear clasps a sun between its jaws
and cartwheels freely through the air
cavorting like a trapeze artist
leaping leisurely from star to star
juggling a dozen different suns
with the adroitness of a skilled conjurer

they waltz above endless pine forests
touching here and there
with their heavy paws
a tree or two that suddenly flares
into a mass of threatening fire
erupting like a raging volcano
that sprinkles the dreamer with sputtering lava

now all hell opens before him
and the terror begins
he feels himself slipping into an inferno
in which he sees his body
bubbling in a ball of fire
his flesh and hair melting
leaving a grinning skull
his eyes burning wrapped in lapping flames
he cowers between the twisted sheets in fright

as the nightmare brings him close
to the razor's edge of waking
the bears appear from the fire
laughing and dancing around his head
and then one by one they retreat
creeping away on tiptoe
as if afraid to wake him
leaving him to settle back into sleep

still dancing they become smaller
shrinking from their shaggy forms
gradually disappearing into the depths
in which they harden into far flung lights
becoming handfuls of scattered stars
thrown across the night's cold face

Before Day Appears

Time   your heart-beat
Palpitates in my hand
It's as black as a bat's dream
Of a cave deep in the side of the moon

You whisper to me
Your secret message
That all roads lead to a solitary star
So distant that I could reach out
And touch it

I hear you chanting
The names of all stars
And one by one
They disappear into the darkness
Leaving swirling holes
Where the peppery hair of the wind fans
Its flames down corridors of memories
Disint egrating in the opening fist of space

Time   I hear you singing
And your song becomes a river
In which the darkness sparkles
Like the glittering fingers of fear
Before the day appears
With its terrible red fins of speed

Night Song

Night with its velvet fingers
covers our eyes
with its sooty touch
and we curl ourselves
into a ball of breathing dust
the size of a child's clenched fist

in my sleep
I sing you a star
a distant star shimmering
among the incandescent depths
and it whispers my song to your ears
luring your dreams into my arms

asleep my heart
a patch of blood
splashed against the night
comes beating at your breasts
announcing the birth of another star

From the Passage of Time

for Chick-Chick

I set my voice against your hair
Addressing that wild bird of distant afternoons
And imagine the long boats gone already
To read the owl's language scrawled
Across the night's face

When the mice return
With summer blazing in their eyes
I watch the rich uncles of my blood openly
Spend their poverty
To amuse a shrinking sun

Now that the slow urchins of time
Somersault through our dreams
The sly tongue of the sea prepares our bed
A cathedral of leaves
In which naked music attends us

Growing thirsty with the sky's weight
We undress our bodies
Gather the evening's milk around us
And voyage among the long grass in our eyes

Memories of Saturday

for Andrew Roland Digby

Et les roses de l'électricité s'ouvrent encore
Dans le jardin de ma mémoire
GUILLAUME APOLLINAIRE

Can you recall
that afternoon
when the evening chose Saturday
say five or six years back

we were making our way
into the city
with all those tangled hair-nets
in our pockets
to examine the mountains

the grass was blushing
in the distance
and small endless lights
kept following us like inquisitive children

punching our way
through fallen clouds
we discovered our first naked hand
folding a transparent bag
full of white mice

wasn't it soon afterwards
that we came across
that bridge whose name
incidentally I forgot
where fabulously wealthy beggars
were selling their beards
for such ridiculously low prices

we bought one
but it didn't suit us
it was either too small or too big
or something was wrong with the colour
anyway I still keep it
in a glass-cabinet
for sentimental reasons
occasionally taking it out
and dusting it

I can also vaguely recall us
tip-toeing past a ruined cinema
and a foal cantering down the steps
with a freshly picked bag of apples for you

we ended the afternoon
having tea in a deserted swimming-pool
the waiter wearing a sailor's suit
two or three sizes too small for him

on our way to the station
you said one day
the light will shine
right through our bones

yes of course it will
I answered
offering my recently washed gloves
to help you across the road

on the train going home
we watched a chicken's leg gallop
across the flooded fields

I remember the photographs we took
how disappointed we were
they showed an empty football stadium
the pitch literally covered with icebergs

as we left the station
it poured balloons
and our names floating inside them
like tiny flakes of lightning
moving under our finger-nails
it was then
that your laughter exploded like sponges

still remembering you
as I lean slightly at right-angles
against this world
I bite into one of the apples
the little foal gave you
and taste the rich music of your laughter

Incident

It was nothing more
than a simple everyday action
I bent down to tie my shoelace
when it snapped

I stood up
holding the two frayed ends

what followed was incredible

trees suddenly uprooted themselves
started whirling about

giant children clambered among the clouds

passing cars sprouted wings and began flying
as if it were absolutely natural

the grass blushed
houses lifted off their roofs and sighed
the sun took out its handkerchief
wiped its perspiring brow
and the moon inexplicably appeared
fanning its flames

I placed the two frayed ends in my pocket
and everything rushed back into place
became all too familiar again

I hobbled on
fingering the two frayed ends having experienced
a step into the depths of the fabulous
without even closing my eyes and dreaming

Story in a Bottle

Something suddenly woke me
around two or three o'clock
that empty hour of the morning
when even dreams refuse
to take shape and materialize

I stumbled over to the window
and discovered the whole house
was calmly sailing into space

I peered down and saw the world
growing gradually smaller
spinning away out into the distance
like a child's lost coloured ball

I raced from room to room
squinting out of the windows
thinking that it was a crazy dream
that all this was impossible
but the house was drifting quietly
like the ghostly Marie Celeste
voyaging into the darkness

I explored all the rooms
finding them singularly silent
all the cats curled up and asleep
not even the bright-eyed mouse
squeaked down in the dank cellar

as I watched the stars
appear and disappear
among the inky depths
like shoals of shimmering fish
I sat on the edge of the bed
and began wondering
if the house had a pair of wings
or a set of billowing sails
as it climbed up among the stars

I was too frightened
to ask myself
who charted its course
or how long the voyage would last

I wrote everything down
just as it was occurring
put the note in a bottle
and hurled it out
into the swirling void
hoping that someone might
find it in years to come
and read my story

The Day America Caught Fire

The day America caught fire
my grandmother woke up
from her long death and
reached up to the sun
and cracked it like an egg

its sluggish blood spilt across the sky
and made a pretty picture
for pavement artists
a few politicians considered it a miracle
the youth of the world cut their throats
and danced in their blood singing
"we are all angels now"

at night drifting between sleep and dream
I imagine my grandmother in heaven
scrubbing God's toe-nails
with a nylon brush and
tucking a wisp of grey hair
behind her ear and saying to herself
"the water's cold and the soap's hard"

if I wake early morning
sometimes I see her ghost
moving among the roses of the wallpaper
and I imagine I hear her
singing to herself an old sea shanty

now that is strange
for we both hated the sea
preferring the City with its winking
night lights staring into dark
like prowling animals

alone at night and in the City with rain
I often catch a glimpse of her
disappearing behind a corner
sometimes I reach out
and almost touch her shoulder

Yesterday's Sun

I open a book
with a flourish
of a rhino's tail
and all the words
become twittering birds
so very dead
that they lay
their eyes again
in our dreams
to help us hammer
nails into sun
caught between
the pages of tomorrow's newspaper

One Night Away from Day

The army returned home wet with sunlight
Isn't Kent the tyrannosaurus county
Where I shall cut off my head and eat it?
The Doctor muttered to himself
How strange and examined the girl again
Climbing into her bed between
The sheets of frozen fog
She had nests of pipistrelle bats
Sleeping under her pillow
A rather elderly gentleman
That's what he called himself
Suddenly walked into the bedroom
And astonished her by removing his heart
Winding it up and wearing it
As a rather natty wrist-watch
Her father was attempting to stand
On one finger in a glass of water
Someone came along and sprayed
The corpse with ink to stop it smelling
But the damn thing barked all night in her bed
As the lovers strolled through the woods
They happened to glance up among the branches
And saw a herd of cows laying eggs
Usually two to four rarely five or more
A few brave people gathered among the trees
But gradually became frightened
Believing them to be agents of the C.I.A.
They reported the matter to the local police
Who chuckled slyly and said "watch us"
And with that remark they majestically
Floated up to the ceiling
While the crowd cowered
In sheer terror beneath them

Sooner or Later

All my neckties
having been happily strangled
by the sweat of the sun
now froth wildly with loud hosannas
like pickled chilblains

sooner or later
they will glove their mouths
with the fangs of the rain running to China
and turn to face the hands of the south
absolutely black with the smiles of lovers

while they hurry along in my pockets
they stand to attention
to polish a virgin's eyes
cupped between her legs
dancing among the tussocks of yesterday

ah my neckties
swan song of hideous crows
they cycle furiously back to their birth
in the teeth of the sun
barking like unlaid eggs

soon they will dance again
among the clouds with the thunder
and rinse their hair with sunlight
hanging from the lips of the lightning

Shaking the Feathers of Sleep

The diamonds yes always the diamonds
Laughing in the straw
With the wind whistling up steam
To drive the left-handed sheep
Over the cliffs of your face
Turning in all directions to meet the sun

I see your hair changing
Its brute intelligence
From blue to red
And green is the colour
Passing through the waters of your sleep
In which you stand
Catching fish in a net of mirrors

O be warned
For I have kissed the fire's sweet lips
And talked with the rain
Hanging inside my pockets
Where two salamanders mate
On the high point of the sun

44

Family History

My wife recently born
prepares her hair for the voyage to her hands
left abandoned in her father's womb
to dry among the sheets of her eyes

she has the lips of a snail in love
the fingers of a tree in flight
the ears of a stone barking at night
the eyes of a ringing table-lamp at sea
the hips of a feathered bush burning in the morning
the legs of the sun embracing itself passionately
the feet of an innocent taxi-cab marooned in her bedroom

with her dreams curled around her sleep
she wakes to bird song
tattooing their notes across her flesh
and takes flight with a flock of Dodos
to the coast of Long Island
where she catches fish with the long poles of her laughter

In a House of Liquid Chalk

To stop
September septembering itself
Out of my hand
I egg my face with the thunder of telegrams
Waking my body of sixty rhino heads
Charging into the wind

Attempting to paragraph a snowball's rage
I tenderly mother my dreams
Into a bed of chimpanzee grunts
To capture the pages of my flesh

I table my feet delicately
Under clouds of pigeons' feathers
Far into the distance
Through the holes of passing gales

In a house of liquid chalk
I stretch my name beyond fields of knots
To portray my skeleton
Standing on the world's rim

Now that the sun's bones
No longer coffin
Themselves in boxes of lost voices
I voyage with my hair where a blow
To the stomach denudes a nun's grin

Van Gogh at Saint Rémy

Unwashed unshaved
            I bellowed at my keeper
"black coffee"
            was up before sunrise
with nothing but the morning star
               hanging solitary
         among the blue depths
I was dressed
        before the birds stirred
               & hammered their songs
       across the countryside
for here was painting to be done
           before the crows
broke from their roosting
          spreading their inky wings
         across the sun
            obscuring its light
what I craved
       was the sun's brilliance
           on canvas
I could feel it
       burning behind my eyes
            my fingers itched
for that intensity
        yesterday I said I'll paint freely
rub some of the violence
         of the inmates here
         into my colours
           spread it thickly
           across the canvas
alone in the fields
        I watch the sun rise
        a blood red phoenix
& wish for its fierceness
         if only I could dip my brush into it

stir its radiance
        into my oils
                my work becomes brighter
        yet it's not enough
I need to touch the sun
        to bring it down
                 splash it
        across the canvas
so that the picture   flares   blazes   dazzles
        even in darkness

Maximilien Robespierre

Slim finger of the stonechat's rage
                              Stone striking stone

Now the long grass of the eye
                              Turns sharply away
                              From the sun
                              And its useless alchemy
Where blood
              Knocks at the abandoned flesh
              Receiving no answer

Ah once
        So many heads were singing
                              Yet burying themselves
                              Beneath the grass
And answering its growth
                    With the language of revolt

For those
        Who moved hills in their sleep
                              The Seine
        Runs from light to darkness
                              Under bridges
Where silence blossoms in caves
                        Where trees reach   stretch forward
To hear the earth's core
                Bubble in ice and fire

For those who fountained out
                    The gold of France
The female sun displays its sex
                    And grins
                    While in games they place
                    Their hands around their necks
To feel the warmth
                    From the candles still flickering
                    In their blood stream
Decaying with its own richness
                    The darkness flows
                    Through their gullets
Returning
         Streaming forward
                    Ebbing back to the body's walls
To begin afresh the circle of decay

Jacques Roux

Stag of rancour
       Of fury
Thrusting violently through the elbow of space
To devour the moving hills
          Hiding
          Attempting to disappear
          Among the breasts of the sun

I witness your terror
Shaking the roots of woman's love
            Where the infinite retreats
            Holding the nerve ends of shattered light

I hear your antlers
Twin branches of fire
         Crush through clouds
         Along underground rivers
In which your blood pursues
The passage of time
        Bandaging its fears against
        The knives of night
        Flashing their smiles
To those who have finished with sleep
Endeavouring
       To escape your wrath

The ice of your eyes
       Destroy
         The world's fires its light
         Stuttering dread among cul-de-sacs
In houses of crystal
Men sit uncomfortably
        Holding out their hearts
        For you to devour
          Wholly and savagely

Louis-Antonine de Saint-Just

Recall the blue of his breast his throat
Turning to gold in time stopped
                          Before birth and after

A hundred years
Two hundred years
Three hundred years
                          Wakes no man's ears
                          To the hummingbird's flight
                          The rapier's sudden thrust through the air

The moon's falling paint
                          Removes his head

It's a difficult time for winter to heal its scars
Scanning its facial rimes
                          In water walking under trees

Sleep against sleep
                          Waking against waking
                          His bones canter to meet the fires
                          In children's cruel games

Tell me
        No man
                Holds out his heart in his hand
                Among the sun's hair
                          Blushing like a whore
Standing astonished in wood
                          Catching fire

Now a dead man rides a horse
Nurses the sick sun
                    And his open wounds foam feathers for bulls
                    To taste with their barbed tongues
                    Blossoming into grunting
                    Swallowing the rivers of France
Leaving only footsteps of blood
                              Across the sky

Jean-Paul Marat

Under the earth's torn sky
                    A tight fist of fury lacerates
                    The throbbing needle of ice in the eye
Stabbing the open breast

                    Once
Silver rode in the mouth
                    In the eye
                              Under the tongue
                                        In the blood
The dark richness strengthening
                              The fruits of France

A woman some call crazed possessed
                              Stumbled into her
                              Diseased vocation

Strangling the sun
              With her smiles
                        Slashing the water's paper breasts
With a jagged blade of moonlight

                    Now the long knife of night wakes
                    And plays cruelly with its broken fingers
                    Teasing the staring eyes

All the Paris trees offer
              Their leafy tongues
                              To lick
              The lolling blood
              Flowing running to water
Where its weaker hump-backed brother
Slouches in a house of muted voices
                              And kisses itself
                              In a flood of crocodile tears

The high-heeled steps of the wind drum
                    Its sculptured sounds
                    Tearing the wind

Now the windows of his eyes are slammed shut
And darkness mingles with darkness
                    Unable to seek a flowing source
                    Of light to escape

Gracchus Babœuf

Rivers tie knots in the air's throat

Someone passes   shadowless   throws ashes
Among collapsing waves in trees
                                        To feed the shy gulls
                                        Sawing the world in half
With their motionless flight

An old woman mocks the naked grass
                                        And sharpens her teeth
                                        With peregrines' tongues
Behind the sun's cold carnivorous face

Decayed before its birth a corpse
Struggles up from its grave
                            Brushes away
                            The earth from under its flesh
And buries its body
                        Before an audience of bored spectators

A dog carries its skeleton between its jaws
                                        Scratches a hole
In the day's forehead
                        To escape the magnet's kisses
                        Poisoning the air

Waking from the waterfalls
                        Below sleep
                        A child idly fractures a stone
With his indifferent gestures
                        Into dead stars

From darkness
        Light appears
                Branching out
                Its fingers to hold the osprey
                Escaping its harsh music
Circling inside its smashed skull

Georges Danton

Fair noise of the clashing of air
>The empty halls of the slow word yes
>Turning stones upside down
>To show their gaping mouths

His words brim
>With spiky blades of grass
>Milking the earth above churches decaying with reason
>Removing their sounds

Drifting like dead deer among hollowed tongues
>>Across the sea's sunken surface

To escape a child's smile approaching gloved night

From the flaming foliage of speech
>The silence seeks
>Its disappearing animals
>Melting into broken mirrors

A sleeping man's eyes gather in wheat fields
>Toys with flowers bending against the wind
>To battle with the city's clawing shadows

Voices of the mob tumble in discarded wine jars
>Pretending to sleep for those already deep in sleep
>Painted with the sun's hare lip

Fallen heads still chatter of France!

Now the sky hides its cunning face to stutter
>Its ringing tones
>Strutting like a naked nun ruined with sex

Among woods where stallions turn from the sun